MW01292984

Buc to Good

The Trials, Tribulations, and Triumph of Being...and Staying...a Pittsburgh Pirates Fan Through the '90s and 2000s.

Jason Zemcik

Jason Zemcik

Copyright © 2016 by Jason Zemcik

All rights reserved. No part of this book may be reproduced, distributed, or transmitted in any form or by any means, including photocopying, recording, screenshotting via electronic reading devices, or any other electronic or mechanical method without prior written permission from Jason Zemcik. The only allowable exception to this is for brief quotations used in critical reviews or certain other noncommercial uses permitted under copyright law.

This book is entirely the author's personal account of the events described herein. The author is not employed by, endorsed by, or otherwise affiliated with the Pittsburgh Pirates. Unless they want him to be. In that case, they can contact him at jason@jasonzemcik.com.

Cover photo credit: Adam Zemcik, 2013 National League Wild Card Game at PNC Park, October 1, 2013.

About the Author

Jason Zemcik is a lifelong Pirates, Steelers, and Penguins fan who was born and raised in Somerset, PA. He saw his first Pirates game, a 5-2 win over the Cardinals at Three Rivers Stadium, in 1989 at age seven and was immediately hooked. His writing about the Pirates, rooted deeply the fan perspective, has been featured on the Pittsburgh Post-Gazette website and MLBCenter.com. He currently lives outside of Raleigh, NC with his wife and daughter.

You can stay up to date on all of his work by going to his website, jasonzemcik.com.

Dedications

To my parents, Ronald and Susan, for introducing me to baseball as a child and letting me stay up late to watch the Pirates so many times.

To my wife Melissa, for supporting me throughout the process of writing this book and encouraging me to share my enthusiasm for the Pirates with the world.

To my daughter Madeline, for making me proud to be a father each and every day, and for sleeping through the entire 2013 Wild Card game at barely a month old.

And to the legions of true Pirates fans who never abandoned ship during all of the tough times – this book is for you.

Table of Contents

Introduction

This isn't a book about baseball.

In no way, shape, or form is the story of being a Pittsburgh Pirates fan for the last quarter century a baseball story. Far from it.

Baseball certainly plays a prominent role, but despite what outsiders and casual observers would believe, getting to the heart of the matter, peeling the proverbial cover off the ball and examining the fan experience of rooting for this franchise during all that it has encountered in recent history is a much deeper matter than simply writing about baseball could ever convey. To try to describe this experience only in the context of baseball would, quite frankly, be to neglect the true story.

The story of being a Pittsburgh Pirates fan for the last two and a half decades, for those who stuck around for all they had to offer, is one of raw human emotion, both positive and negative. It's a story of loyalty and perpetual optimism, all manifest in the attachment of a core fan base to its team that is rivaled by virtually none. These truly trying times for the black and gold showed the true colors of many fans.

There are plenty for whom the 1990's and 2000's are simply a blank spot; the years when the Penguins won three Stanley Cups and the Steelers two Super Bowls. But there are a small few whose belief in the Bucs kept them on board and ultimately brought them to one of the proudest feelings a sports fan can have – saying they stuck with their team through the toughest of times and were there to see it through on the other side, when they were once again winners.

This book is for those folks.

During this era the Pirates played thousands of games. Two will forever be etched in Pittsburgh sports lore. One, a heartbreaking ending that signified the finale of more than just a season; the other, an impassioned statement to the world that the new beginning toward which momentum had slowly been building beneath the radar of nearly everyone but this small group of loyalists, had finally arrived. Two games; bookends to a dramatic tale which encompasses every conceivable element of the fan experience to an exponential degree.

You won't find a whole lot of play-by-play narratives in the pages that follow. The plays were important, but the experience that they all added up to is the real story. For Pirates fans, the real ones who never wavered in their support, this story is one that few other sports fans will ever experience the privilege of calling theirs.

All fans go through highs and lows associated with the silliness that is rooting for sports teams. Everyone finds themselves the butt of jokes and at a loss for explaining their club's missteps on the field in stretches that can span multiple seasons at times. But no group in recent years, and it's not a stretch to extend the window to not-so-recent years as well, has felt it like Pirates fans.

For this group, it became personal. It was a glaring negative mark on their team's, and therefore their own, pride. It was the conundrum of feeling anger at their team when in the company of their own for routinely underperforming, yet staunchly defending them when being laughed at by outsiders. It was blunder after blunder after blunder with no conceivable end in sight, no future that is so often the end goal of rebuilding efforts in any sport.

Buc to Good

The last twenty-plus years offered a road that by all indications, led nowhere, yet one that some still chose to take. While others grew indifferent, apathetic, or worse still, shifted their allegiance elsewhere, this group of fans stayed aboard a seemingly sinking ship. As other teams garnered recognition, highlights, or at a most basic level relevance in Major League Baseball, this core contingent of Pirates fans steadfastly held out a belief that one day their team would be back in the spotlight, for positive reasons.

This book is for them.

And while, as of its writing, the Pirates have yet to ascend all the way to the top of the Major League Baseball mountain, to now be in the same proximity to such an achievement as they were to the bottom for so long is in itself impressive beyond belief for those of us who suffered through so many hopeless seasons to get here. Holding out optimism that this once-proud franchise would again field a team to be proud of wasn't in any way easy, but it was in every single way worth it.

So enjoy this collection of stories; they're my take on this incomparable fan experience, views from taking in games at Three Rivers Stadium and PNC Park, from watching regularly on TV throughout my youth and, in recent years

Jason Zemcik

as life saw me settle away from western Pennsylvania, my computer. They're views that I've found I share with countless other members of this close knit group that saw our Pirates all the way through their journey to get Buc (Back) to Good.

RTJR!

Jason Zemcik
April 3, 2016

Chapter 1 : The End...and the Beginning

One October night when I was ten years old, I cried myself to sleep.

It wasn't a childish fear of monsters in my closet that brought about my tears, but rather a baseball game. I can still recall the scene like it was yesterday, sitting at home in my family's living room watching Sid Bream hobble around the bases to slide across the plate a fraction of a second ahead of Mike LaValliere's tag, giving the Atlanta Braves a 3-2 victory in Game 7 of the 1992 National League Championship Series.

My Dad and I looked on in shock; jubilation in one dugout and agony in the other. Moments earlier I was certain it would have played out the opposite way as the Bucs took a 2-0 lead into the final frame, and I was talking about which night the World Series would start that weekend. Toronto had punched its ticket earlier that day by defeating the Oakland A's for the American League pennant. I was already surmising how the Bucs would have a competitive advantage in their familiarity with the

Blue Jays' David Cone, formerly of the National League East division rival Mets, which could allow them to steal one of the early games.

But there would be no such matchup. Silence now permeated the room while on TV a raucous Fulton County Stadium crowd cheered their Braves' improbable comeback. My Pirates were *that* close to playing in the World Series, yet now I was left with an off season to wonder about what could have been, what should have been. Little did I know that the loss that night was only the tip of the iceberg.

In the years that followed, I'd actually be left with much more time to wonder, more time to feel the angst of a proud baseball town thwarted. The game's economics drove our star players to one by one depart the Steel City for greener pastures, leaving the Bucs a shell of the franchise that I had fallen in love with during their run of three straight N.L. East titles in my early days as a baseball fan.

After a few minutes it was upstairs to bed. It was a school night mind you and I was up late. I closed my door and waited just long enough for my Dad to make his way down the hall to my parents' room, then buried my face in my pillows and bawled. These were *my* Pirates and seeing them lose the way they did tore me apart.

I had watched every game that year, lived out that pennant-clinching moment in my backyard wearing my Andy Van Slyke #18 jersey a million times over. I was so captivated by those Pirates that I took every t-shirt and baseball cap I owned out of my dresser, placed them in a box, and set them next to our basement door so I could simulate my own experience right down to the detail of pretending that I was donning championship shirts and caps in the clubhouse after the game just like the players did.

I was undoubtedly one of countless kids and kids at heart for whom the taste of a World Series berth was so painfully close that night. Now it was all gone, washed away in the fleeting moment that it took Bream, a former Pirate as well as one of the slowest players in baseball due to multiple knee surgeries, to dash home from second.

In retrospect, we didn't know how good we really had it in the era that preceded that heartbreaking defeat, even though Lanny Frattare flat out told us so. I don't remember the opponent but do vividly recall his words one summer Saturday afternoon during the 1991 campaign. I was listening to the game on the radio when Frattare, a staple of my youth as was Mike Lange during the winters, mentioned in the casual way that broadcasters bring things up between pitches, "Pirate fans are really fortunate to have another outstanding club this year."

Even at a young age it was a statement powerful enough to get my attention. I thought about how I had just started watching baseball the year before and, as if it were supposed to happen that way, my team finished in first place in the N.L. East right out of the gate. Granted, they lost in the playoffs to the eventual World Champion Cincinnati Reds, but it wasn't a bad way for a kid to break into following the game. And so as I lay in my bed and the tears continued to flow into my pillow, thoughts of waking up the following day with my team in an entirely different place for a long time to come didn't even cross my mind. The present moment stung too much, and even if I would have had the gift of immense foresight, at that age twenty years held absolutely no context.

I didn't give any thought to why baseball worked the way it did on the adult, meaning money, side of things. I didn't ponder why players making millions would end up leaving Pittsburgh for more millions, or why the Pirates wouldn't pay however many millions were necessary to keep this team intact for one more shot at World Series, having no understanding of the fact that it wasn't an unwillingness but rather an inability that was the issue.

All I was thinking about as night turned into the wee hours of the morning was how Bream managed to make it all the way home from second base fast enough on a bad knee. How Jose Lind, our reliable Gold Glove second baseman, booted a grounder a few plays earlier to give the Braves runners at the corners instead of recording one more out, one of a number of peculiar events in the game's final innings that would ultimately haunt us. Or most perplexing, how Francisco Cabrera, who had barely appeared in double digit Major League games that season, could come off the bench in such a pressure-filled situation and calmly drive in the winning run like it was a spring training exhibition.

However it all happened though, it did; and it was the beginning of a twenty-year run of consecutive losing seasons for the Pirates that still stands as the longest such streak in North American major professional sports history. The years that ensued were, to say the least, largely forgettable. All the optimism in the world couldn't replace reality; this was a franchise that simply became stuck in the proverbial basement, try as it might to climb out. Therein lies perhaps the most fitting beginning to the story of loyalty that rooting for the Pirates represents. So many people look at that fateful night in Atlanta as the end of an era. The last time the Pirates contended. The last time they mattered, actually.

For some fans though, it was also the beginning of a journey that gave us thousands of opportunities to abandon ship, that tested our devotion and patience, and that would ultimately bring us through an experience that few if any other sports fans could relate to.

Chapter 2 : This Just Doesn't Feel Right

It was a feeling similar to that when a football team jumps offside on a fourth and inches hard count. The one where, as the age-old saying goes, "Everyone in the stadium knew it was coming and they still got 'em!"

After a host of off-season departures in the wake of the '92 NLCS heartbreak brought about by the small-market, and thus small-budget Pirates being unable to pony up the high-dollar contracts that so many of their stars commanded on the open market, the 1993 edition of the Bucs looked decidedly different from what fans had grown used to in recent years. And, logic dictated, as that different look included a number of younger and less-experienced players complimented by a few older veterans looking for a home to extend the twilight of their Major League careers, the team's position in the standings was in for a different look as well.

There was the false hope, mostly strong homerism more than anything else, that somehow the Bucs could manufacture success with a small ball type of roster and avoid the tumultuous falloff that losing the likes of Barry

Bonds, Bobby Bonilla, and Doug Drabek over the past two winters would bring about. A 3-0 start and a .500 April teased some into actually believing it was possible, but even the strongest optimism couldn't replace the reality that the '93 club just wasn't the same as those of the previous three years. Before long the old football adage rang true as the team stumbled to a 75-87 mark, finishing a demoralizing 22 games back in the very division it had so recently owned.

And while everyone knew it was coming, it still hit like a ton of bricks.

Perhaps most emblematic of the Pirates moving in a different direction was their decision to part ways with both members of the battery that became forever etched in Pittsburgh sports lore for their role in the Bream play the year prior. Less than a month into the campaign they released LaValliere. A few months later reliever Stan Belinda, who gave up the hit to Cabrera that scored Bream, was dealt to the Kansas City Royals at the trade deadline for two pitching prospects, Jon Lieber and Dan Miceli. The optics of both departures weren't lost on anyone. Intentional or not, both could easily be viewed as an attempt to eradicate the bad memories of the year before that was disguised as part of the rebuilding process.

LaValliere was largely, no pun intended, a fan favorite during his time in black and gold. Fans hardly blamed him for his role in the NLCS loss. If anything, the agonizing image of him diving across his body in an attempt to tag Bream, his glove falling just inches shy of what would have been an out if he were over six feet tall, seemed to resonate with many Pittsburghers who saw a bit of themselves in his stocky build and all-out effort. But despite his release, the Bucs were still responsible for the bulk of LaValliere's $4 million guaranteed salary that year, so parting ways with him didn't do much in the way of clearing payroll space to begin retooling for the future.

Belinda on the other hand wasn't met as kindly by the Pittsburgh faithful in the aftermath of the previous year's playoff heartbreak. He had pitched admirably throughout the '92 campaign where he assumed the closer role full-time, and was put in a difficult situation in Game 7 to say the least, being called upon in the ninth inning to hold a 2-0 lead with the bases loaded and no outs. But such is the reality of sports fans; always in need of someone to blame, be they deserving or not. In that instance, Belinda wasn't.

Although Lind booted that sure out a few plays earlier, and although backup right fielder Cecil Espy misplayed a fly ball down the line turning another routine out into a double for Atlanta's Terry Pendleton, Belinda's was ultimately the "name on the door" as the man standing atop the mound when the final run was scored. And so midway through the '93 season he was out the door, many around town still holding feelings of angst toward him and doubts circling whether he would rebound and play a relevant part in the team's long term plans making it that much easier to see the upside to the trade.

All around, the '93 campaign delivered a vastly different brand of Pittsburgh baseball; one that was uncomfortable, unfamiliar, and, most notably, uninspiring. Bob Walk led the pitching staff in wins but had a losing record. Al Martin, the heir to left field in the wake of Bonds' departure, topped the club in home runs with a tally that was barely more than half of what Bonds hit the year prior. When summer turned to fall and the Bucs were mathematically eliminated from playoff contention with weeks remaining on the schedule, barely anyone batted an eye. As captive an audience as they had had in the Steel City during their run of prominence, they now faded quickly into irrelevance. For so many fans who had invested their emotional energy into the club in recent years it was disheartening, and about to get worse.

The following season the Pirates turned in a similar performance in the standings. Even the brief excitement of hosting the Major League All Star Game, which went down as one of the better midsummer classics in history, an extra-inning win for the National League, couldn't mask the reality that fans' descent into indifference as it pertained to the Bucs was well underway. And with anger and apathy spreading rapidly among baseball fans everywhere due to the looming, and ultimately realized, possibility of a players' strike, they plunged further into oblivion among the local sports scene.

Although pegged as catastrophic to baseball on a national scale, the strike, which cancelled the end of the regular season as well as the playoffs and World Series, didn't actually seem to matter to many Pirates fans at the time. The Bucs were once again nowhere near a playoff spot, so suffice it to say their absence for the last few weeks of the summer wasn't a disruption to a ton of sports lives. When they returned in 1995 however, the work stoppage resolved, they were greeted by an opening night crowd that had finally reached a breaking point. After a particularly horrendous sequence in which the Pirates surrendered multiple runs to the Expos and probably couldn't have made any more throwing errors if they were legitimately trying to, fans pelted the Three Rivers Stadium turf with the plastic flags that were the evening's souvenir giveaway.

It was at this juncture, now essentially two full seasons into this new brand of Pirates baseball, that the fans appeared incapable of holding back their true state of mind any longer. Or more aptly, their true emotions, as so much of what would materialize both on that opening night and in the coming future was fueled by lingering frustration that didn't appear to be going anywhere any time soon. Apathy had turned to anger; anger over a combination of still-unresolved feelings about the '92 NLCS defeat, over the inability to keep the team's high-priced stars as much as their unwillingness to give the Pirates the "home team discount" despite professional sports from a business perspective simply not working that way, and anger over the previous year's strike as a matter of principle simply because of what it represented and not as much for how it impacted Pittsburgh.

Ultimately though, Pirates fans felt anger over the fact that this was now their baseball team for the foreseeable future. For as good as the early '90s were in Pirates baseball, the mid '90s, now in full swing, were equally as bad.

Moreover, they just didn't feel right for this proud baseball city.

Chapter 3 : They Might be Bad, But They're Ours

It's one of the nuances of how life just works that seems to apply to nearly every type of group that people associate with. Politics, religion, family, relationships, and of course sports fan allegiances; all are subjects where the time-tested rule of thumb is that it's alright to make fun of your own, but an outsider better not dare do the same. Such was the disposition of the Pirates faithful in 1996 when rumors that the team was poised to be sold and inevitably relocated began inching toward reality.

A group backed by the City of Pittsburgh had stepped in a decade earlier to purchase the team in the wake of the 1985 clubhouse drug scandal and financial fallout when a sale and relocation had also seemed likely; a stop-gap measure designed simply to salvage the Pirates' residency in Pittsburgh until a buyer could be found. Now a decade later, local cable television magnate John Rigas had his proposal to buy the club rejected by Major League Baseball. Rigas was the city's choice to assume ownership because of his pledge to not move the club, but his proposed deal relied too heavily on equity in the team and prospect of selling stock in lieu of more cash up front for the league's liking. With the Rigas deal out it appeared that so too was any chance of the Pirates remaining in town. Given the developments of recent years though, the prominent question coming from most outsiders, baseball fans or not, was simply, "so what?"

So what if the Pirates left Pittsburgh? They now stunk, and, due to baseball's economics had little prospect of getting better any time soon. Attendance at games was steadily declining, caused in equal parts by their ineptness on the field and the field's ineptness itself, as dated concrete and turf multi-sport cookie cutters like Three Rivers Stadium has fallen wildly out of style in the '90s in favor of beautiful baseball-only stadiums like Camden Yards and the new Comiskey Park. Couple those factors with the the Penguins and Steelers fielding competitive and popular teams during the same era and a sale of the Pirates to an out-of-towner would seem to barely register a blip on the radar beyond its immediate newsworthiness.

Sure, from a practical standpoint fans shouldn't have cared if the Pirates were on the brink of being gone. Shouldn't have cared if the summers would now be entirely consumed with the Stanley Cup playoffs and the countdown to Steelers camp. At least that's what any unassociated, objective individual might have to say. In the eyes of true Pirates fans however, it was the exact opposite. They still wanted their Pirates in town. Just like you still love your kids, your spouse, and your best friend even when they're getting on your last nerve, so too did these fans love their Pirates deep down. And while it took the prospect of losing them to really bring out these emotions in people, when they did come out they were genuine.

It was at that juncture that so many realized losing baseball games would be temporary, however long "temporary" might actually mean, but losing their team would be permanent. It was apparent that true fans did in fact want a buyer to commit to not moving the team. While they wanted a new stadium as well, they also wanted the Pirates more and likely would've settled for remaining in Three Rivers. But that type of logic doesn't enter into negotiations over sports franchises where millionaires and billionaires are trying to reach agreements with each other, and so for the Pirates it was new stadium or gone.

My personal recollection of that time in Pirates history was one fraught with nerves; a different variety of nerves from when Belinda was on the hill against the Braves a few years before. In that scenario it was a minute-by-minute sort of nervousness, but in this case days would drag on with no developments. Not exactly ideal for a junior high student that fortunately had little in the way of real-world worries on his mind yet and thus could spend his days not paying attention in school and instead anguishing over what was to happen with his baseball team.

Those thought sessions always followed a similar pattern; wishing I knew the full details beyond what the news would provide, in an era where the 24-hour Internet news cycle had yet to be born. Thinking that somehow the City would magically come up with the money to make all of the grown-up problems go away, then hearing my Dad explain that to build a new stadium someone had to pay for it, and when the team was losing, getting that "someone" to be each and every individual Pittsburgher wasn't a hard sell, but nearly an impossible one.

Plenty of others saw it that way too, for as strong as their desire to keep the team in town was, the matter of "how" was quite literally, the million dollar question that the past year and a half and multiple failed proposals couldn't answer. A Major League Baseball club could definitely be a good business investment for any potential buyer, albeit somewhere else. Suffice it to say when a guy in his early 30's from California surfaced as an interested party, most fans' initial reaction wasn't exactly one of optimism.

But surprisingly, newspaper heir Kevin McClatchy's vow was to keep the Pirates in Pittsburgh. An enthusiastic baseball fan in his own right, McClatchy inspired hope in Pittsburgh fans because he saw beyond the current state of affairs, almost as if he were one of them. He saw the franchise's proud history that in his estimation there was simply no alternative but to keep intact. He saw the loyal fans' hope, however dim, for a brighter future. He had aspirations of a new ballpark as beautiful as any of the others that had become all the rage. This position drove him to assemble a group of investors that would bring the financial means to the table and to also work through the process with City officials to spearhead his vision of how to make the Pirates' new home a reality.

And so, as good fortune and plenty of hard work would have it, McClatchy's offer was the one that Major League Baseball embraced and ultimately approved. I can vividly remember the newspaper headline the day after McClatchy's group finalized the deal, which included plans to fund the construction of a new stadium: "They're STAYING Pittsburgh Pirates!"

Pittsburgh fans knew little about Kevin McClatchy when he emerged from the group of would-be buyers as the one who ultimately assembled the right mix of cash and commitment to hold the franchise and its city together during one of the most trying times in its existence. But what they did come to know through the tumultuous experience of nearly losing the team was that all anyone who bled black and gold really wanted was a pledge that the Pirates would remain in Pittsburgh, through thick and thin. McClatchy delivered this, at the time when it was most sorely needed.

The Pirates weren't very good on the field when Kevin McClatchy assumed control of the organization, and they didn't get much better throughout his tenure. But the franchise endured, survived, and remained *our* Pirates as a result of his efforts, which for all of the losses on the scoreboard was an emphatic victory.

Chapter 4 : Magic Among Misery

That whole 20 years of losing thing? Few outside of Pittsburgh remember that it almost didn't happen that way. History almost didn't remember the Pirates in a category all their own with regard to consistency in losing, because the '97 edition of the club almost *did* the unthinkable. This ramshackle bunch nearly won the N.L. Central title, baseball having gone through divisional realignment by that point, despite being expected by many to lose well over 100 games due to the vast inexperience on the roster. Instead of living down to their expectations however, this edition of the Pirates nearly shocked the baseball world by pulling off a feat that would have rivaled any sports upset of historic proportions.

After the all of the feel-good hype surrounding McClatchy's purchase of the team had died down, it quickly became time to get down to business leading up to the '97 campaign. First on the agenda was slashing the already-slim payroll by more than half, meaning a full-fledged fire sale of the previous year's roster. Names like Jay Bell, Carlos Garcia, Orlando Merced and Jeff King, some of the last remaining holdovers from the division championship teams of the early '90s, were off to new homes. In their place was a squad whose *combined* salary was less than a handful of Major League stars' *individual* paychecks, at roughly $9 million.

The team featured, to name a few, a young Jason Kendall, a younger Jose Guillen, a guy (Kevin Polkovich) who was moonlighting as a grocery bagger at the beginning of the season while chasing his baseball dream in the minors until injuries necessitated his call up, a guy (Tony Womack) who would go on to have a solid decade-plus Major League career but was an All Star that season clearly for no other reason than because every team had to be represented, and a smattering of other castaways who, quite frankly, would've been on minor league rosters in any other organization.

But this group that was dubbed the "Freak Show" for its hodge-podge yet successful nature, this team that was led by a "Joker" as third baseman Joe Randa was affectionately known due to his omnipresent smile, just kept proving week after week, month after month, that it was actually for real. Playing in a poor division helped of course, as the Bucs "winning" ways actually ended up as a losing season by a handful of games. Even still, nobody really expected them to hang with the eventual champion Astros all the way up to the final week of the schedule.

And though the little engine that almost could ultimately ran out of steam, the '97 campaign was a vast departure from the previous few and gave fans plenty to be proud of, even if it was obvious that the group that took the field that year was in no way the long term solution, but rather a mere stop gap of bargain-priced players.

There was little thought of the future that year for Pirates fans, as the present held so much to be enthusiastic about. The '97 summer was clearly a magical one, bringing about a three game home sweep of the White Sox and their superstar slugger Frank Thomas, and highlighted by one of the most memorable games in Pittsburgh baseball history. Francisco Cordova and Ricardo Rincon teamed up to pitch a combined 10-inning July no-hitter against the very team the Bucs were chasing for the division title, the Astros. In addition to the tandem pitching gem, the victory was capped off by a mammoth walk-off homer by Mark Smith which sent the Three Rivers crowd into a frenzy the likes of which rivaled those early '90s playoff games.

That game was a microcosm of the season for those Pirates; an improbable, unfathomable, and electrifying night that saw them find a way to grind out a victory. I remember thinking to myself as I watched, from nearly the same spot in the living room of my childhood home where

I suffered through the finish of the Bream game, that no hitters just weren't the type of thing we were able to experience as Pirates fans in those days. They were displays of pitching mastery we expected to see from the likes of Hideo Nomo and David Wells, not anyone on our Pirates staff.

But inning by inning, as Cordova continued to blank the Astros with McClatchy cheering from his customary spot in the first row behind home plate, the feeling of watching something special unfold that has few parallels in other sports grew and grew, similar to the feelings that the Bucs evoked throughout the season. When Rincon tossed a scoreless tenth and Smith delivered his heroics at the plate, a division title seemed every bit a realistic possibility for those Pirates, even if so many were still trying to convince themselves that what had happened that night, and what was happening during the season, was reality.

That '97 Pirates' season largely gets forgotten among all of the other mishaps that surrounded it, glossed over as just an anomaly in an otherwise consistent era of losing. But for one magical summer, the Pirates weren't the downtrodden, forever-rebuilding club that they were known as during the rest of the '90s and 2000s. They were the type of club that made me take a radio on the bus for a school field trip so I wouldn't miss an afternoon game one day when our teacher clearly didn't check the schedule in advance; the kind of club that made all of the predictors and pundits look like fools, and made logic go out the window as they defied every ounce of conventional wisdom in their pursuit of a division championship.

Unfortunately, as uplifting as they were though, they were also the kind of club Pittsburgh wouldn't see again for a long time to come.

Chapter 5 : Few and Far Between

I often wonder what happened to that guy.

Not in a grave sense of course, at least hopefully not. Just more of a "what he's up to these days" kind of sense. I didn't know him from Adam, and still don't, yet I think of him often. I think of the fleeting moment we shared and the connection we made. I think of the humorous looks it drew from others in the vicinity and the absurdity, yet genuineness of it all. I think of this guy, a gangly-looking fellow with a scruffy five-day shadow and hair in a ponytail under his cap, a complete stranger that I'll most likely never see again, and the ten seconds or so that we were entirely on the same wavelength with respect to what was going on around us.

A little deep for a baseball book, you're thinking? Possibly; though I cautioned you up front that this book isn't really about baseball.

It was August of 2003 and the Pirates were taking on Clint Hurdle's Colorado Rockies at PNC Park. What got both myself and my temporary friend furiously high-fiving in the left field rotunda, just happening to be in the same place at the same time despite having never before met was, laughably enough, a victory by a team that at the time was six games under .500 over a club that would go on to finish the season 14 games under.

Hardly cause for celebration, except that it was a Pirates win, and we were both Pirates fans. True Pirates fans. When the Bucs' Mike Lincoln got Rockies' outfielder Jay Payton to ground into a game-ending double play with the tying run 90 feet from home to secure the 1-0 win, for one brief moment records and standings didn't matter. In that instant nothing mattered other than hearing the "New Pirates Generation" song come over the PA system and seeing the Parrot break into his victory routine.

Exuberant flashes like that were hard to come by in the 2000's, and so were fans like that guy. Hard to find yes, but they were out there; and they were the ones that really banded together during this stretch, which is why just happening to be in the same place with someone like-minded was special. Someone else who still got fired up over this team. Someone else who still jumped, literally, at the opportunity to celebrate the Bucs coming out on top in dramatic fashion even if they were still firmly entrenched at the bottom of the standings.

There were others like him, if you looked hard enough. There was the guy that I met during a game against the Angels in 2004 who could best be described only as "a guy who a guy like me would talk to about the Pirates," meaning he was an anomaly by still being every bit as much of a die-hard fan then as he was back in the days of the Killer B's. There was a sellout crowd on hand at PNC that night, plenty of people drawn by the novelty of interleague play but only a fraction who were likely to also be there when the regular variety of scheduling resumed and familiar opponents such as the Cubs, Cardinals, and Reds continued their rotations through town. As we chatted he delivered a premonition that I wholeheartedly shared, yet absolutely knew put both of us in the minority.

"It'll happen again," he said, with a tone to his voice that made it clear he was harkening back to the Bucs' successes in the days when satin snap-up jackets were still considered stylish dugout wear. "It might not be this year, or next, but it's going to get better." While I absolutely believed him, the realist in me knew that our opinion was founded on nothing other than blind optimism. The Bucs were now more than a full decade into the rebuilding process, and nobody with an ounce of sense was actually calling it that any more, "rebuilding" having given way to just "being bad." Loyalty and reality weren't mutually

27

exclusive, at least not for me, so while still staunchly supporting them deep down I questioned how long it would truly be until they'd put a winner on the field again.

I had jokingly dubbed the Bucs of those days "Major League Baseball's farm team," due to their penchant for having young talented players develop into big league stars who commanded big league star salaries and promptly departing for other teams. Nowhere was this more evident than in 2003, when both All Star Game starting pitchers, Esteban Loaiza of the White Sox and Jason Schmidt of the Giants, were former Pirates.

So as the losses on the field continued to mount up, driven largely by the losses on the roster, this "call me crazy" sub group of us, fans who had committed long ago that we were in it for the long, no, the longer haul, really needed each other. We needed others who wanted to get excited about anything positive rather than bemoan the nearly everyday negatives that had become the club's calling card. We wanted to tailgate when we came to the ballpark and have blinders on as if every game was a one-game season. Deep down we knew that it was the only way we could find anything rewarding in the drudgery that brought down so many who once rooted for the Bucs.

Buc to Good

As I was filing out of the stadium after another disheartening loss, this time at the hands of the Mariners in another "come one, come all" 2004 interleague game a few weeks later, I could only chuckle. The choice of music to serenade folks on their walk out showed that at least the stadium entertainment guy had a sense of humor about the Bucs' plight. Lenny Kravitz's "Again" emanated from the PNC Park speakers, clearly intended to be a jab at the thousands who wouldn't be back any time soon:

"All of my life
Where have you been?
I wonder if I'll ever see you again
And if that day comes
I know we could win
I wonder if I'll ever see you again."

Shortly after, in a watering hole directly across from the ballpark, I got to chatting with another of my kind. We both had jerseys on, both perked up when in the first minute we detected each other's die-hard tone about the night, the season, and the general state of Buccos baseball. I told him flat out how I wished more people would just get behind the team even if naïvely; better to be happy about what we had than be angry over what we didn't.

He responded by telling me that he'd been a regular at games since he was a kid in the "We are Family" days of

Stargell, Parker, and Tekulve and that after experiencing that era, and the Bonds-Bonilla-Van Slyke regime as a 20-something like I presently was, he'd gained a perspective that put him somewhat at ease amidst the Bucs' current woes. "Sports are cyclical," he opined, showing a depth of thought not usually found in a bar as the clock neared midnight. "Sooner or later it's gonna come back around our way, we just gotta hang in there until it does."

In an odd way his words brought me satisfaction not only that night, but through the years that would follow. Actually, recollection of all of my interactions with these types of fans did. Sports are cyclical. Fans are too. And while the paths of each tend to diverge during the bad times, the law of the game seemed to always hold that sooner or later they had to meet back up. For the time being, that was what those of us who were committed to our Pirates had to go by. But hearing it from others, however few of us there may have been, made it much easier to believe in.

I often wonder if just by sheer chance I'll ever see any of those guys again. Whether they realized it or not - they likely didn't - they helped me make it through the tough times on pure hope of one day again reaching the days we knew could win.

Chapter 6 : They Built It, But...

There are elephants in rooms, and then there was this.

When the Major League Baseball All Star Game, a celebration of our national pastime that doesn't just recognize the game's biggest stars but is also, perhaps more so than in any other major professional sport, an acknowledgement of both the game's history and its future, returned to Pittsburgh in 2006 it may as well have brought the entire Barnum and Bailey's pachyderm crew with it. While there was plenty to talk about during the three-day extravaganza, one of the great aspects of mixing fans of all different clubs, there was one simply unavoidable topic that made fans of the host Pirates cringe each one of the million times it came up.

Beautiful new ballpark, maybe the best in the majors. Yet nothing to show for it.

The feeling was akin to that of defending a friend who you knew had messed up. Trying my best to put a positive spin on the Bucs current state though there really was no such thing. The team stunk, no two ways about it. Had for a long time. And here they were, providing the backdrop for the entire baseball universe to celebrate against. Talk about uncomfortable.

The last time Pittsburgh played host to the Midsummer Classic in 1994 at Three Rivers losing was still a new feeling. The Pirates were only two seasons removed from the string of three straight division titles. There was a sense that getting used to a rebuilding process that might take a while, a realization that the team wouldn't contend for the foreseeable future. But coupled with those feelings was the assumption that, as sports rebuilding processes go, the Bucs would gradually make progress and before long be a contender again. Needless to say it was a bit awkward when "a while" was still going on and that future still wasn't any more foreseeable when the All Star festivities returned a dozen years later.

There was no hiding the fact that the deciding factor in bringing the game back to Pittsburgh so soon was PNC Park. With elements of Forbes Field incorporated into its design and the right field Clemente wall 21 feet high, all in tribute to the team's rich history, it opened to great fanfare in 2001. It represented the fruition of Kevin McClatchy's vision and commitment to the city and the fan base in delivering where other potential ownership candidates faltered.   It was a cornerstone of the city's overall revitalization, driving development of the surrounding area and providing a fresh facelift to this no-longer-an-old-steel-town that most of America still knew only as "an old steel town." Unfortunately though as the Bucs proceeded to christen their new digs by losing an even 100 games in its first season, it also represented a harsh reality – new stuff can get people's attention for a while, but it can't hold it.

Even a local radio station did a skit where "going to the Pirates game" was a euphemism for going to dinner at PNC Park, the punchline being "Wanna go to the Pirates game tonight?" "Nah, I'm not hungry." In other words, saying that folks would go for the attraction of the beautiful new stadium, to grab a bite to eat and take in the magnificent view of the city skyline in the outfield, and then leave after a few innings without actually paying any attention to the game. To borrow a catch phrase, it was funny because it was true. PNC's main life at the turnstiles in the 2000's was the "just something to do" crowd as the Pirates couldn't regularly attract the actual Pittsburgh sports crowd due to their ineptness.

There were some individual bright spots during those years, some standalone outstanding moments turned in by the likes of Jason Bay, Brian Giles, and Freddy Sanchez. There were flashes of brilliance that reminded folks of the Pirates of old brought about by solid play from Jack Wilson, by now and then quality, dare I say almost dominant, pitching performances by Oliver Perez and Zach Duke and even Kris Benson, an enigma in and of himself during his time in Pittsburgh. But two things there weren't throughout the PNC years. One of them, of course, was wins. The other was consistent attendance.

With the All Star Game coming to town I was determined to be there though. An Army Lieutenant recently home from a tour in Iraq, I begged and pleaded until the Major I worked for finally relented and let me take leave mid-week to make the eight hour trip from Fort Bragg, North Carolina to Pittsburgh despite having just been home on leave a few weeks prior. I reciprocated by getting a ball autographed for his son, at the time a Little Leaguer whose game was showing a lot of promise. Throughout batting practice one night Alex Rodriguez lingered for nearly an hour close to the throng of fans I was among down the left field line, but wasn't in much of a signing mood. Jonathan Paplebon was much more receptive to fans wanting to commemorate the event, thus his signature it was.

There were plenty of nice folks that descended upon PNC during the course of the two nights, the Home Run Derby and the game itself. Plenty of good baseball people that knew those of us who stood by our Bucs were going through a rough spot. But even their kindness, their willingness to not rub our failures in, just made for an awkward feel. A sense of "they're only being nice about it because we're so bad."

I met one guy who even swore that Pittsburgh was so far down we'd welcome back public enemy number one, Barry Bonds, if he wanted to don black and gold again. As I countered by saying Bonds was the very embodiment of the Pirates' current plight, the face of superstars exiting stage left for contracts a cash-strapped small market franchise like ours couldn't afford, and that the fans would never in a million years entertain the thought of wanting him to return, the guy stopped me in my tracks with one of the most straightforward statements I'd ever heard. "He'd at least put people in the seats, even if it was to boo him. They're playing in an empty stadium every night, what could it hurt?"

That was one way of thinking about it.

While there was no actual talk of going after Bonds, out of lack of interest by both parties and the fact that his salary at the time was nearly half of the Pirates 2006 opening day payroll, the thought that someone had actually brought it up as a plausible option in the same vein as Jose Canseco making cameo appearances throughout the minors simply to bring fans out to otherwise dead ballparks made the situation all the more clear. All of baseball felt sorry for us.

I couldn't exactly say I blamed them. On that trip home a few weeks prior I invited a buddy from Texas to tag along. He was a big baseball fan who had never been to Pittsburgh but wanted to check it out after hearing my incessant rambling about all it had to offer. We took in a Sunday afternoon game against, conveniently enough, his Astros in which the Bucs carried a 4-0 lead into the 9th yet managed to surrender four runs to force extras. The Astros promptly plated one in the top of the tenth while the Bucs went quietly in the home half to lose 5-4.

As the crowd filed out uneventfully, he observed "It's almost like they expected it to happen this way," noting the lack of any emotion that manifest itself throughout the group. He was exactly right; the days of expecting anything less than disappointment were long gone. An extra inning loss where we held a 4-0 lead a half hour earlier? Add it to the tab.

When we returned for the All Star Game a month and a half later it's as if the rest of the out-of-towners present could sense that same hopelessness among the Pittsburghers. And while playing host to the festivities was a nice distraction from what July in Pittsburgh, at least in a baseball sense, normally meant, it did little to mask the frustration that was so evident on all of our faces.

I wouldn't go as far as to say we were to the collective point of rallying behind the "Bring Back Bonds" guy's idea, but honestly, we were in search of something, anything to get this team to matter again. Seeing fans from other cities turn out and immersing ourselves in "the rest of baseball" for a few days, witnessing the excitement of fans whose clubs were in pennant races just made it hit home that much harder how far away we were as Pirates fans. Hearing chatter about what their respective clubs needed to do in the second half of the season, what moves they needed to make at the trade deadline that didn't involve "dump salaries" just made us upset, and everyone could sense it.

Yes, during those two days when Pittsburgh was home to each of Major League Baseball's 30 teams the Oakland A's may have had an elephant emblazoned on their jersey shoulder patch, but on the collective prime time stage, the Pirates had a gigantic one tramping around PNC Park.

Chapter 7 : Temptation and Torment

One of the most beautiful yet at the same time confounding things about sports is that so often outcomes can be summed up as simply fitting. No other adjectives needed to describe the events that unfold or, more specifically, the oddity, unlikeliness, and irony of them. Just fitting.

2011, nearly the two-decade anniversary of the Pirates' sharp left turn to incompetence, seemed about as fitting as ever could be a year to finally bring about a reversal in fortunes. By this time the playoff drought had taken on a life of its own, making headlines as it approached the longest ever among all of the four major professional sports. But in recent years the Pirates had quietly, beneath the radar of the national media and even the not-so-closely watching eyes of a large portion their hometown followers, been assembling a crop of players who inspired hope that they were capable of doing the unthinkable and finally pulling the team out of the rut it had been stuck in for so long.

Fitting then, that this year things were showing more than just a scant glimmer of being different than the eighteen that had preceded them. Fitting that when the All Star game arrived they were not only above .500 for the first time since 1992 but also sent three players to the contest for the first time since 1990, the start of their previous era of success. Most notably though, it was fitting that their first appearance on an ESPN primetime telecast in nearly two decades came that season in, of all places, Atlanta.

July 25th, a Monday night, under a muggy and drizzling Atlanta sky, was to be the Bucs' coming out party. A chance to show all of baseball that they weren't just another rendition of the same old Pirates. That they were the group that had finally turned the corner, the team that was finally poised to atone for the years of misery endured by its long-suffering fan base. A chance to exorcise the demons that still haunted them from the Turner Field parking lot, a concrete expanse that in a former life was the site of Fulton County Stadium.

This night, and on a larger scale this series against the Braves, represented the prime opportunity for the Pirates to emphatically make a statement that they were indeed back. In the first game they did exactly that, waiting out a two-hour rain delay to stymie the Braves en route to a 3-1 victory. But in a cruel yet ultimately fitting way, the following night's game proved to not be nearly as kind.

Deadlocked at 3-3 through nine innings, the teams remained as such through the equivalent of two complete games, surpassing the six-hour mark as the home half of the nineteenth commenced. As Tuesday night turned to Wednesday morning, the game began to take on an air of eeriness. No longer an ordinary pedestrian contest, the notion that it was going to be one of those games that gets remembered meant that inevitably thoughts of exactly *how* it would be remembered began to creep into the minds of every Pirates fan, this one included, who put off getting their rest in the name of sticking it out alongside their team.

For better or worse this game, much like the Pirates' performance of so many previous years, was of the stuff that mainstream news is made of. Noteworthy in its difference from the norm, significant in its meaning more so than just your average run of the mill weeknight contest. Not unlike that of another Wednesday game, in another Atlanta stadium, some nineteen years ago.

How fitting then that it was a play at the plate of all things that decided that contest and largely, the season. A landmark game that ended in a Braves victory after a runner was ruled safe at home. Ruled, in this case, because Atlanta's Julio Lugo scored the winning run from third on an infield ground ball when replays clearly showed he was out. Afterward umpire Jerry Meals admitted that he had blown the call, an assessment that Major League Baseball conferred with albeit with little recourse to reverse.

It must have been something in the Atlanta sky, something in the invisible zone surrounding home plate in a Pirates versus Braves game, that led Meals to inexplicably extend his arms and call Lugo safe, giving the Braves the victory and taking the collective wind out of the Pirates' sails. From that point on, the season wasn't the same. While one loss does not a season make, this one dealt a devastating blow strikingly similar to the grand scale setback that the '92 NLCS defeat had rendered.

For the remainder of the year the losses piled up. The Bucs slipped in the standings, falling well out of contention for both the division title and Wild Card spot. Talk of making the playoffs turned to talk of just hanging on to finish above .500, neither of which happened. It was a level of insult to injury that was beyond comprehension. The sheer irony of it all seemed to reaffirm that the franchise really was cursed, that the Braves were the root of the hex, and that try as they might and with the remaining fans rooting as they might, there was still no escaping the label of a loser stamped upon them by the events of 1992.

Until the following year, that was.

In 2012 feeling of a first place club at the halfway point of the season with an All Star and MVP candidate who was near the top of the league in nearly every offensive category patrolling the outfield wasn't new to Pittsburgh, though it did take a significant bit of mental dusting off to recall the last time such was the case. A harkening back to when Barry Bonds, the former, was still skinny and Andrew McCutchen, the latter, was just a kid. What required more of a dusting off though were Pirates fans' feelings after the collapse of the year prior.

As the summer wore on and the Bucs continued their winning ways, people slowly became convinced that things were different this second time around. The club was a year more experienced and, most significantly, a year angrier after letting their grasp on a playoff spot slip away in 2011. No way that it could happen again this season. No way lightning could strike this beleaguered franchise two years in a row after all it had been through.

Until it did.

First place quickly turned into second, which wasn't all that bad considering a Wild Card spot was still in tow. But like the cash that was still going out the door to Derek Bell long after he had famously shut down in 2002, that also slipped away, and before long the results of losing nearly twice as many games as they won during the pivotal months of August and September left the Pirates in a familiar spot, below .500 and, not that it needed to be mentioned, out of the playoffs. For a city and a team that had been subject to every sports catch phrase there is to describe devastation, this was by far the worst yet. It brought with it a maddeningly compounding effect, missing the playoffs the way they did in the same season that officially locked up two consecutive decades of losing.

In the final game of the year, one that meant absolutely nothing to the Bucs as well as their opponents that day who were already playoff-bound, manager Clint Hurdle did something out of the norm that resonated for a brief positive moment with the Pittsburgh faithful on an otherwise gloomy day, both literally and figuratively. In deference to all that he had accomplished that season, both statistically and in the larger sense of carrying the club in

44

the now seemingly-impossible quest to return to relevance, Hurdle pulled McCutchen from centerfield mid-game to give the contingent of fans who remained at PNC an opportunity to acknowledge him as he left the field.

It was, if you wanted to look hard enough, one miniscule bright spot in what was an abhorrently dark ending to the season. Maybe it was just as simple as Hurdle trying to do the right thing even if few would recognize it. Or maybe he really did have the managerial resolve to weather the inevitable storm that would be coming over the off season, a barrage that after the previous year's identical collapse would figuratively be as bad as a January Pittsburgh blizzard.

Not long after the classy tribute to the Bucs unquestioned leader between the lines by their leader in the dugout, the game ended uneventfully. The Pirates departed the field for the final time in the 2012 season, each player to scatter to wherever the offseason would take them. The other squad, to board a plane home and get ready for the playoffs. Nothing all that noteworthy, except for exactly which team it was that officially closed the door on the Pirates most disappointing campaign in a run of disappointing campaigns.

Yes, walking off of the other side of the PNC Park field that day as everyone in black and gold wondered if this quandary would ever be solved were none other than the Atlanta Braves.

And of course, it seemed only fitting.

Chapter 8 : It Feels So Good to be Back

Given the years of hopelessness in the rear view mirror and the recent years of pure torture so fresh in so many minds, nobody faulted Pirates fans for adhering to the old "fool me twice" adage when approaching the 2013 season. Not even when, as spring turned to summer, the Bucs were again right in the thick of the N.L. Central race. Not even when they held the best record in the Majors through June, a month that saw the much-anticipated Major League debut of prized right-hander Gerrit Cole. Cole's first game, a victory over the San Francisco Giants, was everything the Pirates fans could have hoped for and then some, as in addition to regularly hitting the upper 90's on the radar gun he helped his own cause by driving in two runs.

Still nobody faulted those who just weren't buying it when the Bucs' Major League best record was still intact through July, or even when they survived August, the bane of their previous two seasons, to remain one game ahead of St. Louis for first place in the Central. Quite frankly, after what this club had done to them over the past two seasons it wasn't a stretch to say that Pirates fans still wouldn't believe it was for real right up to the very moment of seeing a playoff berth secured.

So when the Bucs took the field in Chicago on September 23, 2013, it was only natural for plenty of fans to carry an air of skepticism with them even with the prospect of finally capturing that long-awaited playoff spot becoming a reality. The Bucs had rid themselves of the "winning season" albatross a few weeks earlier, locking up their 82nd victory of the year on September 9th, but by this point it simply wasn't enough. It was playoffs or bust this time around, and given the hard luck of the previous two seasons, fans were still expecting bust until they saw otherwise with their own eyes. A win that night however, coupled with a Washington loss to St. Louis, would make it real. With a win and some help, decades of "one of these days" talk would be erased.

In the time that had passed between the current day and the distant memory of winning Pirates clubs past, I had literally experienced an entire generation of life events. I got my driver's license. I graduated from high school. I graduated from college. I fought in two wars. I got married. I bought a house. And, just three weeks earlier, I became a father.

7,649 days to be exact. The longest playoff drought in major professional sports history. 7,649 days of having to grin and bear it as a fan. 7,649 days of our team being the butt of jokes from other fans, the media, and even people who knew nothing about baseball other than that we'd been really bad for a really long time. I was 31, a far cry from the child that sobbed in his pillow that October night two decades ago, yet at heart, the exact same fan.

With the game tied 1-1 left fielder Starling Marte, who the year prior had been a large part of the promise that abounded before the pain set in, captivating Pirates fans by hitting a home run on the first Major League pitch he faced, did the same in the top of the 9th to give the Bucs a one-run lead. The stage was now set for closer Jason Grilli as the Cubs came to bat in the home half of the inning.

There are moments in sports where we can see symmetry between situations so clear that it amazes us, and at this point, this game delivered one of them. The Bucs carrying a tenuous lead into the bottom of the ninth on the road. An opponent managing to get a man on and then following up with a perfectly-placed knock to the outfield, as the Cubs did when Nate Schierholtz reached on a fielder's choice and Ryan Sweeney dropped a Grilli offering into shallow right field. A moment of pure symmetry between the

Bream game in '92, between the Lugo game in '11, as Schierholtz was waved around third in that this game which had the potential to mean so much to the Pirates and their long-suffering fans was culminating in a play at the plate.

As Schierholtz made his dash for home I almost couldn't believe what I was seeing. *"Not again. Please not again!"* I thought to myself in the split second it took him to slide and Pirates' catcher Russell Martin to apply the tag.

Just like that, the game concluded. I stood in my living room lit only by the glow of the TV, much the same as I did as a childhood Pirates fan on the first night of many that it all went so wrong. This night's contest had indeed ended in nearly identical fashion to that Atlanta game some twenty years ago the other one two seasons earlier, in a flash of a moment where I held my breath and could do nothing other than let loose pure, raw emotion as I saw the umpire emphatically make his call.

Except this time, it was different.

This time the emotion that spilled over from Monroeville to McKee's Rocks, from my native Somerset to Squirrel Hill to the ends of the earth where Pirates fans I met in the

Army were pulling for the black and gold from afar was of a different variety. Of a form we collectively had been waiting and waiting and waiting to let out so bad we literally didn't know what to do with ourselves.

Out!

Long-time Pirates play by play man Greg Brown, who had called multitudes of disheartening and downright dreadful games during his years as the voice of the modern-day Bucs, captured the moment by exclaiming simply, "What a finish! Unbelievable!" Moments later the final score from St. Louis posted: Cardinals 4, Nationals 3, and the celebration was officially on. The Pirates, *our* Pirates, were going back to the playoffs! After so many agonizing, painful seasons, the wait was finally over. The scene that night was one for the ages. Champagne being sprayed wildly about the Wrigley Field visitors' clubhouse. Brown with a victory cigar in the broadcast booth, his on-air partner John Wehner, a member of that 1992 Pirates club, by his side.

The Pirates were the talk of the sports world the following day. The story of how the franchise that forever couldn't finally did, told in media outlets and over water coolers everywhere. There were celebrations throughout western

Pennsylvania that lasted well into the early morning, many of them also making national headlines as the stories and the people behind them were every bit as riveting as the on-field script.

People such as Kenny Meier of Windber, PA who was in high school during the infamous '92 NLCS and spent the 20 years since the Bream moment feeling as if a piece of the Pirates experience he once knew had been stolen. "I had a love affair with baseball and the Pirates from an early age, hearing stories from my Grandma about going to World Series games at Forbes Field and watching games myself at Three Rivers," he said. "I felt sick in the aftermath of Game 7 against the Braves. Losing the way we did and then realizing that game was the last time so many of the stars of my childhood would ever touch a baseball in a Pirates uniform just cut so deeply and lingered for so long. But these Pirates made it right again."

2013 was finally the realization of what die-hard Pirates fans had known for years would someday take place. Throughout the season the Bucs' newfound success prompted lots of fans to come back, which was great.

But some of us never left. That was priceless.

Chapter 9 : The Blackout That Ended All Dark Days

Try as they might, no writer or broadcaster could truly hit the nail on the head, or in a more fitting analogy connect squarely with the fat part of the bat, in their attempt to describe the night in Pittsburgh sports that many thought they'd never live to see. Perhaps the best summation of the scene came from an entirely unassociated rock band, one with Ohio ties ironically enough given the evening's opponent, as O.A.R.'s song "This Town" presented the closest-to-perfect words to capture the feeling of such a long-awaited night.

"This town, this night, this crowd
Come on put em up
Let me hear it loud
This town, this city, this crowd"

From the time the gates to PNC Park opened right up to the first pitch by Pirates starter Francisco Liriano against a backdrop of Jolly Roger-waving fans, there were hardly words to do the scene at 115 Federal Street justice other than simply stating the obvious.

This town. Home to this crowd. Fully deserving of this night, more so than any fan base in all of sports. It was a night which they'd waited through three different U.S. Presidents, two of them two-termers, to behold. Indeed, it was nothing short of pure bedlam on the North Shore as the 2013 National Wild Card Game against the Cincinnati Reds got underway.

And then, the playoff-starved Pittsburgh faithful kicked it up a notch further.

Dubbed "The Blackout" as the Pirates wore their popular alternate jerseys and their fans followed suit in dark attire, it was a rebirth, a cleansing, and a new beginning. It was something that no outsider, nobody who hadn't faithfully suffered through the post-Bonds, Bonilla, and Van Slyke 90's and the "no other way to describe it than awful" 2000's and definitely not through the collapses of 2011 and 2012 could truly understand the significance of. Playoff baseball in Pittsburgh again? Even those witnessing it in person couldn't entirely grasp the reality of what was taking place. That's how far down this franchise once was.

Even though the Pirates had wrapped up their playoff spot over a week before, an "I'll believe it when I see it" attitude befell nearly everyone who bled black and gold, as if it could somehow be unjustly taken away in the same manner as they had felt robbed many times before during their record losing streak. But this time it was for real, the Pirates had made it back. Back from the depths of the Major League Baseball basement, from regular 90-loss seasons and twice hanging a century mark in the 'L' column since their last postseason appearance. Back from a year, 1995, in which they were the only Major League club that didn't even draw a million bodies through the turnstiles.

When a disgruntled group of fans organized a mid-game walk out during the 2007 season to protest the team's years of inadequacy, when the Pirates lost a game 20-0, yes *twenty to nothing* to Milwaukee during the 2010 season, when each one of a cornucopia of other shortcomings occurred over the years it was nearly impossible to imagine that there would ever be a day when a meaningful game would be played at PNC Park in October.

So as Doug Drabek took the mound to deliver the ceremonial first pitch, his sandy locks of years prior now showing a touch of gray to further illustrate just how long it had really been for Pittsburgh, as TBS led off its broadcast with cameras spanning the fanatical scene in the far reaches of the upper deck where there was barely even a spot to stand let alone an empty seat, when it all finally came to fruition, that's when the realization truly hit home for those of us who are part of the special fraternity of fans who hung around through all of the dark days.

This was about more than baseball. Way more.

When I watched that October night play out, from my living room couch as a barely three-week new Dad, and vicariously through my brother who was in the stands at PNC, I knew I wasn't alone in my feeling. There were droves of folks, across western Pennsylvania and scattered throughout the world even, for whom the significance of the Pirates' return to prominence held a meaning far deeper than just a first round playoff game.

I remember the exact moment that my wife really got it. She'd known me for several years by that point, realized my loyalty to the Pirates in the first few weeks after we met, but in an instant of true revelation said, "This really means something to you, doesn't it?" as we stood at our kitchen counter and I rattled off for the thousandth time all the peripheral factors that made this first Pirates playoff tilt since I was in elementary school something for the ages.

It was more than a baseball game. More than a playoff contest with a spot in the Divisional round at stake. It was an end to anger, frustration, and bitterness, some of it warranted, some of it not, most of it simply the product of proud fans who were fed up and wanting someone, anyone to blame over the years. It was an end to being the butt of jokes among other fans, especially prevalent for those of us whom life had transplanted to other locales, and an end to always being the last spot if any at all on the national sports highlight reels.

That was the true significance of this game. For the segment of fans who intertwined their identity with their city and their teams, and continued to do so throughout one of the absolute worst stretches of professional baseball ever put together by any team, it was the end of a twenty-year embarrassment.

It was finally a long-awaited chance to be proud again.

And to say that the Pirates obliged would be like saying Niagara Falls is a small tributary. Liriano was dominant, scattering four hits across seven innings and keeping

Cincinnati hitters confused throughout. As he strode calmly off the mound after each frame the actuality of what was happening grew increasingly stronger. Three up, three down. An occasional baserunner here and there, but no damage done. Somewhere around the fifth inning it really began to sink in. The Pirates weren't just in this one, they were in control of it. They had entered a zone where no amount of history or bad playoff vibes from the past could stop them. And while Liriano made it real in his dominance, it was the Bucs' offense that truly made it timeless.

Marlon Byrd, a late-season veteran acquisition playing in the post season for the first time in his career got the barrage started with a solo homer in the second inning. Before the fans even had a chance to catch their breath, Russell Martin, an offseason free agent signing who, in coming to Pittsburgh from the Yankees served as another symbolic representation of how far the organization had come, followed suit two batters later launching a pitch deep into the Pittsburgh sky that also came to rest in the frenzied crowd. Appropriate respect given to Jack Buck, the offensive outburst by the Pirates only fueled the surreal nature of an evening that had the entire baseball universe "not believing what it just saw."

Almost the entire universe.

Everyone except the Pirates fans that had dutifully hung around through the dark years, who knew that someday, no matter how far off it seemed, this night awaited them. A night that couldn't entirely atone for their years of frustration but that could come pretty close. A night that existed only in their minds, only in the time they spent daydreaming, for so many seasons.

As the game progressed the crowd took to heckling Reds starter and perennial All Star Johnny Cueto in a manner usually reserved for hockey goalies. As the slow, irksome chants of "KWAY-toe....KWAY-toe....KWAY-toe" emanated from the stands, increasing in volume and in passion with each round, the seminal moment of a seminal night happened, a bit of highlight reel footage that will live forever in Pittsburgh. Cueto, about to toe the rubber to deliver a pitch, dropped the baseball.

Yes, the Pittsburgh crowd shook a veteran Major League pitcher's nerves so badly he literally dropped the ball. For as many ways as a writer could try to cleverly explain that one, there just aren't any. Something magical was truly afoot on this much-anticipated evening; the Pirates could do no wrong while the Reds, a fine enough team to their own credit, simply could do no right. Exhibit 946 (if anyone was counting) came on the very next pitch, as Martin belted Cueto's offering into the stands for the second Pirates homer of the night. If the party was on in Pittsburgh at noon that day it became epic when Martin rounded the bases to the deafening PNC Park roar.

By the time closer Jason Grilli recorded the final out of the game and longtime play by play announcer Brown delivered his famous "Meet me in St. Louie!" call to tell the world that the Bucs were moving on to the next round and a date with the Cardinals, Pirates fans had entered a state of euphoria never before known to many of them and so long forgotten for others. To put it into perspective, there were college kids who in their lifetime had only ever *heard* of the Pirates once being good. There were grown men and women who hadn't seen a playoff victory since they were in elementary school. Truth be told, the chance to play another round in the playoffs that season, while important, was all icing on the cake.

As the fans poured out of PNC Park, no longer the nicest yard in baseball that had never hosted a game that mattered, there was revelry that made New Year's Eve look like a Monday at the office in the Pittsburgh streets. It was a scene that rivaled a Steelers Super Bowl celebration, complete with a guy stripping to his shorts and jumping off of the nearby Clemente Bridge (he swam ashore just fine) in celebration.

The 2013 Pirates would push the Cards to the brink before ultimately falling in a deciding Game 5 of the Divisional Series in St. Louis. In contrast to their last playoff elimination, hardly anyone was the least bit upset other than for the immediate moment. What took place in the 2013 campaign was beyond remarkable, beyond historic, beyond riveting. In retrospect, it's easy to say that October 1, 2013 was a night the long-awaiting Pirates loyalists will never forget.

A more accurate statement is that it was everything they had always imagined it would be.

Chapter 10 : How Far We've Come

While there would never be another 2013, never another all-around magical experience that held the significance of the year prior, when the Pirates embarked on 2014 the question of what the club would do for an encore burned in the minds of everyone who had gone on the incomparable journey with them over time. All of the Wild Card euphoria, the shackles cast aside, the weights lifted; all of the other platitudes to describe the tremendous accomplishment that was finally cracking the playoff code a year removed, the following season's Bucs proved to have something just as significant up their sleeves, albeit much more subtle.

The 2014 club seemed to pick up right where they left off the previous year, opening the campaign with a dramatic extra inning walk off victory against the Cubs. Hometown hero Neil Walker's home run in the bottom of the 10th that sent the largest regular season crowd in PNC Park history home happy, and in the games that would follow 2014 saw several more bright spots for the Pirates. Notable among them was infielder Josh Harrison having a breakout season that saw him advance from reliable yet marginally-known utility player to first-time All Star. Harrison's hustle and energetic attitude fit perfectly wherever in the lineup manager Clint Hurdle placed him and his defensive reliability was a much-needed upgrade at third base, left vacant by the team's decision to experiment with converting Pedro Alvarez to first base given his defensive woes at the hot corner.

As the year rolled on the Bucs hovered in and out of playoff contention, a second straight postseason berth never seeming overly likely yet never falling too far out of view. Such is baseball, where so much of success lies in a club's ability to stay close enough throughout the grind of the six-month schedule and then peak at the right time. And peak these Pirates did, playing better than .650 baseball in September to erase their deficit in the Wild Card standings, though not enough to surpass the Cardinals for the N.L. Central title.

In an interesting parallel for a team whose journey over the past year had been rife with them, September 23 again brought with it the possibility of securing a playoff berth. It was another "win and get help" scenario, and the Bucs lived up to their end of the bargain, claiming a 3-2 victory while the supporting act to last year's post-season drama, the Reds, carried out the other prerequisite by defeating Milwaukee.

But it wasn't merely the act of punching their playoff ticket for the second straight year that held so much meaning to the Bucs, it was something deeper. It wasn't even the manner in which they took care of business that night, the victory lacking the final-out tension that the previous year's playoff clincher had. What was of most significance on that night was where it all happened, and who it happened against. For the first time since the early '90's the Bucs were again a back to back playoff club, and the clinching victory came in, of all places, Atlanta.

What was that earlier part about some things in sports just being fitting?

If the previous year's success was a cleansing, celebrating in Atlanta represented a full whitewash of any lingering remnants of negativity. An exoneration of the hauntings that had followed this franchise around during its run of failures. The scene of so much disappointment 22 years before, the place where the champagne was on ice in the visitor's clubhouse only to be carted away at the last minute, now represented a new chapter in Pirates baseball.

Buc to Good

On this particular Atlanta night there was no 9th inning tomahawk chop from a sold out crowd that spurred their Braves on to a comeback, just a strong collection of "Let's go Bucs!" cheers from the Pittsburgh contingent that could be heard throughout the otherwise empty ballpark. The fact that the Braves' season was long over other than the requirement to play out the remainder of the schedule made the night just a touch sweeter.

For a Pirates club so starved for success, in a venue that for so long was representative of all things bad, the celebration, much more subdued than that of a year prior, was more than warranted as it brought about further closure to the previous bleak era of Pittsburgh baseball. It was a chance for the Bucs to embrace their transition from Cinderella feel-good story to a group that had now proved it wasn't a fluke. A club that instead was beginning another run of successes, and ultimately a team whose new place in the Major League pecking order was in the company of other consecutive playoff participants.

For the players it was a further boost to their confidence as they continued to author the franchise's evolution. For the fans it was sweet vindication after the events of decades past. All the way around, it was more than just a playoff clincher; it was a major milestone for an organization that

65

was coming into its own and forging its new identity as a winner. And in a satisfying sort of way, it was the beginning of a trend where reaching the playoffs became less and less needle-moving each year.

The 2015 campaign didn't feature the same Opening Day fireworks as the year prior but did further show the Pirates to be a bona-fide contender. That edition of the Bucs was buoyed by the offseason return of right-hander A.J. Burnett, so instrumental in guiding the 2013 club to finally knock down the playoff wall, as well as a victory in the bidding war for Korean superstar Jung-ho Kang who would prove a vital cog in the offensive machine to help offset the departure of 2103 playoff hero Martin to Toronto. Mark Melancon came dominantly into his own, assuming the closer role full-time in the wake of Jason Grilli's trade to the Angels the year before, and setup man Tony Watson became known as the toughest 8th inning pitcher in baseball, rarely surrendering any ground in preparing the slate for Melancon to put the finishing touches on a Pirates victory.

Those victories were aplenty as the '15 Bucs quickly established themselves as being among the class of MLB as the summer progressed. The only problem was that their classmates were none other than their divisional neighbors, the St. Louis Cardinals. As gratifying as it was to hold the second-best record in baseball for much of the campaign, it was equally frustrating for the only team the Bucs were looking up at to be one they had to outpace for the Central title. The highlight of the season was a July series in which the Bucs took three of four from those very Redbirds in Pittsburgh, two of the victories coming in dramatic walk-off fashion on back to back nights and one in front of a national audience on ESPN's Sunday Night Baseball. While their record would be good for the top spot in any other division in the league, and the chase of St. Louis was very much alive at the midway point of the season and well into September, it ultimately fell short.

When September 23rd rolled around in 2015 and a Wild Card berth again was up for the taking, it's as if the Pirates were seasoned pros at the whole deal. Mostly because by now they were, which was a beautiful thing to those who had been on board for the team's entire journey. The opponent for Act Three of their playoff clinching performance was the Colorado Rockies, and this time around there was no rushing out of the Coors Field dugout after the final out was made. No mobbing each other on the field or wildly popping bottles of champagne in the clubhouse afterward. 2015's playoff celebration, if you can even call it that, consisted merely of a small toast.

That's right, a toast. If the ability to remain low-key is representative of personal growth in life, the same can absolutely be said for the maturation of a baseball club. These Pirates had most definitely done this before. Add to it the fact that, consternation over the Cardinals being a thorn in their divisional side notwithstanding, the 2015 campaign was the club's most successful since that infamous '92 run, and it was a remarkable spot to be in. Five years earlier not many would've thought the Pirates would be holding a postgame toast to acknowledge making the playoffs for the third straight season. Not many would've realistically thought that players would be talking about the club's sights set far beyond just getting to the dance when in the fairly recent past just finishing .500 was a pipe dream.

Mine is just one of the "never thought I'd see the day" stories that Pirates fans everywhere were able to take an extraordinary level of pride in. After the years of frustrating debacles and empty seats at PNC Park, the Pirates were now strolling into the playoffs for the third straight year and acting like it was just another day at the office, because it was. When the Pittsburgh faithful realized that their Pirates were one of only three teams, those same Cardinals of course and the L.A. Dodgers being the others, to make the playoffs in each of the last three years there was a collective sense of pride felt well beyond the confines of the three rivers.

St. Louis., L.A., and Pittsburgh. That had a pretty nice ring to it.

For the better of twenty years the Pirates unrivaled futility put them in a league all their own, one that was legitimately not even Major League caliber baseball. Now they were sharing the company of the Cardinals and Dodgers, two of the league's most consistently successful franchises of late. This group of Pirates had graduated from feel-good story to full-fledged contender, and watching the maturation process unfold over the years, both at an organizational level and individually in so many of the players, was nothing short of remarkable.

For each and every Pirates fan who stuck around during the dark years, these were truly special times indeed.

Chapter 11 : Recipe for Resurgence

So how does a long-suffering sports franchise really find its way out of the doldrums? Find its way back to relevance after being the league doormat for so long? Break its reputation as a brief pit stop at best, a death sentence at worst, for any career?

Sure, there are the clichés. Develop young players. Be aggressive in free agency. Add the missing pieces. But when you're *that* far gone, and moreover when you were on the brink of being back twice only to fail miserably both times, what's the real answer, if one even exists?

Hold that thought, we'll get to it. But first...

How does the marketing staff of a long-suffering sports franchise come up with a way to promote it? When the product is that terrible. When fans have been let down time and time again, for as long as some of them have been alive. How do they, with straight faces, offer up anything in the vein of convincing fans to spend their hard-earned cash to come out to the ballpark when the end result is more than likely going to be disappointing?

Giveaways are fun, especially for the kids. Postgame concerts draw a good weekend crowd. On-field antics, inclusive of racing ethnic foods, are downright hilarious for brief moments. But in the end none of them bring people to the ballpark on a sustainable basis. None of them sell jerseys, or hats, or certainly not season tickets. At least I don't recall many saying they were jumping to renew their seats in 2008 so they could get the first crack at seeing Sauerkraut Saul 81 times a year.

Two dramatically different questions, each rooted in entirely opposite aspects of the business of baseball, and carried out by different arms of the organization. Different challenges and constraints, different obstacles to overcome. Different yet equally long roads to reach two different yet so similar desired outcomes: a winning team on the field, and fans in the seats to watch it.

As it went for the Pirates, somewhere along the line someone in the PR department coined a phrase. Who knows whose brainchild it really was or how much or little debate there was over using it. Who knows if it was laughed at even on the inside, knowing that if it became the label of the club it absolutely would draw jeers on the outside. Who really knows? They went with it anyway.

Pride. Passion. Pittsburgh Pirates.

That became the team's new marketing tagline after a decade and a half or so of losing, at a time when it was hard to draw any of the first two from the club. It of course was met with all of the chagrin that one would expect, but nonetheless, it remained.

Back to that original thought though, the one about how the actual team on the field turns things around. As mystifying as it may seem, it was that same marketing tagline that held the answer to righting the on-field ship.

Pride. Passion. Pittsburgh Pirates.

While two or three pieces do not an entire roster make, there are certain roles on any sports team that need to be filled, that must be filled, for the team to be a success. In the state this Pirates franchise was in, those roles had to be filled by individuals who did nothing short of exude the characteristics that represented success to an exponential degree. And while there were hundreds of draft picks and free agent signings and trades and a handful of managerial changes over the team's extensive run of losing, one by one the three pivotal pieces fell into place and the club started looking up.

Pride.

A.J. Burnett came to Pittsburgh on the tail end of a career that saw him win a World Series ring and amass largely impressive stats. A veteran who, prior to joining the Bucs, had pitched in a number of places, most recently on the game's biggest stage in its biggest media hotbed. For a guy from Arkansas, life as a Yankee had its ups and downs. A no-hitter, the aforementioned World Championship, but also the constant scrutiny of the New York scene.

The one thing that Burnett was so well-known for from an intangible standpoint throughout his career was the one thing the Pirates so desperately needed in a pitching ace. Pride. Pride in the team, pride in the city, pride in the effort put forth day in and day out. Most importantly, pride in being a veteran leader of the club, in showing younger players the right way.

The Pittsburgh fans embraced him for it from the onset. It was as if he had always been one of their own, fitting right in and giving them as much of a belief that a change in fortunes was eminent as he did his teammates. They appreciated his blue-collar ways and his desire to be there wearing the black and gold. He appreciated their support and acceptance of his quirks. A perfect marriage, and the cornerstone of the team's successful push to get over the playoff hump in 2013 after multiple failed attempts.

A one-year stint in Philadelphia in 2014 only brought about a desire to return to Pittsburgh, and so the man who had acquired the nickname "Batman" over the course of his career came back in black for one more ride in 2015. One more season alongside many of the men who he helped groom into winners for the franchise's first time in what seemed like eternity two years earlier.

After tossing his final pitch as a Pirate late in the 2015 season in a game against the Cincinnati Reds, retirement looming in the offseason and no guarantee of a post season start due to the possibility of a one-and-done Wild Card, Burnett departed the PNC Park mound to a lengthy standing ovation and acknowledged the Pittsburgh crowd with his signature cap tip that had become a fan-favorite during his tenure. It was a demonstration of the pride he felt for his time in Pittsburgh, a pride that had been severely missing prior to his arrival but now ran strong in this baseball town reborn.

Passion.

Clint Hurdle could've managed the Mets. They came calling just as the Pirates did in the winter of 2010, seeking an architect for a rebuilding effort just as challenging. Hurdle chose Pittsburgh though, the baseball opportunity aside, for its proximity to The Children's Institute which could provide world class healthcare for his daughter, who was born with a rare genetic condition known as Prader-Willi Syndrome that causes low muscle tone and often excessive obesity in children.

Family first. For Hurdle it was as true in life away from the diamond as it was on, where he got his Pirates to buy in, to care about each other, and to make every day count by playing with passion. He knew from the start it wouldn't be an easy road, but he was up to the task. When the 2013 Pirates finally secured the franchise's first winning season in the last twenty there wasn't a single person in black and gold; player, fan, or otherwise; who would say Hurdle's positive, caring, and above all passionate way of commanding the on-field operation wasn't to credit for finally accomplishing what all before him since Jim Leyland had failed to do.

The passion for his family that led Hurdle to Pittsburgh in the first place was the same passion that led him to get every last ounce out of a club that was "ounce-less" upon his arrival and made him another of the cornerstones that finally pushed the Pirates over the hump.

Pittsburgh Pirates.

Can't-miss prospects are only that until they miss. Or until they become missed, in the case of those that get groomed and traded away. The Pirates went through their share of each over the years.

But there was this one kid from Florida.

One of the multitudes of "can't miss" talents that are pegged as the next generation of Major League stars every draft season, Andrew McCutchen officially became a part of the Pittsburgh Pirates organization in 2005 when they invested their first pick in his speed, both of foot and with the bat. His swing was effortless yet powerful. His range in the outfield remarkable. They'd seen others with many the same attributes work out less than ideal, yet still they took McCutchen. Must've been something about him.

In 2009 he became a member of the Pittsburgh Pirates at the Major League level, being called up in the midst of another losing season when another summer fire sale vacated the starting center field spot. From their first impression the fans knew he had something special. Over the seasons to follow McCutchen continued to develop as a player, showing his talent with both the bat and the glove, and perhaps just as importantly, his commitment to the franchise that had dubbed him as their "can't miss" pick despite every reason to be gun shy given their prior track record.

By 2012 Andrew McCutchen had become the face of the Pittsburgh Pirates franchise. A six-year contract extension signed in spring training was the formal part, but it was McCutchen's presence in black and gold, his signature smile and penchant for delivering spotlight-worthy performances that made him known around the league, not just around the three rivers. In the seasons that finally saw the Pirates play in October, McCutchen dazzled per his usual; walk-off winners, diving catches, and who could forget moments like the one where he handed over his batting gloves to that kid in the gold Pirates throwback jersey in the center field stands in San Diego, the "I love you man!" highlight reel playing over and over on ESPN.

In the process of becoming a Major League star Andrew McCutchen became the very embodiment of the new Pittsburgh Pirates, the third lacking piece during all the challenging years before.

Pride. Passion. Pittsburgh Pirates.

In the end a winner on the field can sell itself, and all it took to accomplish both was a simple slogan that formed a blueprint the entire franchise could build itself around. Turns out those marketing folks weren't as crazy as everyone may have thought after all.

Chapter 12 : It Comes with the Territory

What does a guy who had a lifetime spring training batting average under .100 and never played in a regular-season Major League game during stints with the Padres, Mets, and Royals know about the Pirates run to resurgence? Quite a bit actually.

As Garth Brooks so aptly put it, the Pirates could've definitely missed the pain brought about by the briefness of their playoff runs in both 2014 and 2015. Could've avoided the hurt of the one-game "win or go home" setbacks caused by the unfortunate luck of having to go up against each year's respective post season buzzsaw on the mound in the Giants' Madison Bumgarner and the Cubs' Jake Arrieta. As good as the Wild Card was to the Bucs in 2013, it was equally bad in both '14 and '15. But if that were the case they would've had to miss the dance, to borrow a phrase from Brooks.

Frustrating as each was to behold, a mere few hours of Bumgarner and Arrieta dominance didn't take away what Pittsburgh baseball experienced over its most recent, and that feels good to say, run of three consecutive playoff seasons. Which isn't to say that just making the Wild Card game each year became height of fans' aspirations and expectations for the Bucs simply because they were so bad for so long. Just being there clearly wasn't enough in a city where celebrating participation trophies is expressly verboten, by directive of one of its most illustrious football stars. But it absolutely was worlds better than where Pirates baseball was ten years prior, which was almost packed up and moved out of town at the worst and so far on the outside looking in that it took high-powered binoculars just to get a glimpse of a pennant race at best.

I think back to my experience at the All Star Game in '06, when as I mentioned earlier one of my most striking observations was the joy with which other teams' fans viewed their season. The enthusiasm that came from just "being good" even though most of them wouldn't win the World Series, or even get past the first round of the playoffs. Some wouldn't even make the playoffs, but when you're still in the hunt until the end of the season, or nearly the end, you have something to get excited about.

That's where the Pirates finally advanced to in 2014 and 2015. And while the result in each campaign illustrated that they still had plenty more steps to take in terms of realizing their on-field potential as a ballclub, for their fans it was still possible to be happy about being back in the mix again without being happy for only that. Possible to still despise the pain that could ensue if another year in the vaunted N.L. Central resulted in another Wild Card game and heaven forbid another unlucky draw of the year's hottest pitcher while at the same time relishing in the joy of the dance. Or perhaps more succinctly put, being proud and staying hungry weren't mutually exclusive.

Just like nobody could take away the magic that was the 2013 playoff run, no amount of pondering or rationalizing could negate the fact that the 2014 and 2015 Pirates were outplayed in the Wild Card format and had their seasons ended as a result. Each was still a very good baseball team, but each played a particularly bad baseball game on the night that it needed to have its best stuff in order to not be looked at as somewhat of a disappointment through the microscopic lens of the playoffs. For the '15 club it especially stung, as so many believed that group was built to take on anybody in baseball, capable of winning it all. Unfortunately though, because they didn't best the Cardinals they were forced to pack up and move out after one loss, when a handful of other teams with worse records at least got a best-of-five playoff opportunity.

And honestly, even though an infinitely-viable argument can be made against the justness of the Wild Card format, the more compelling stance to take is simply that disappointments such as 2014 and 2015 come with the territory of being a good team. Exiting the playoffs early, losing games that were much-anticipated and much-hyped are, unfortunately, the not-so-fun part of being a perrenial contender. Having to deal with the downside of playoff disappointment comes with the territory of being in the mix; it's the pain that comes with the dance. And dancing is always better than being left on the outside looking in, even if your team isn't the last one left on the floor.

Will this current generation of Pirates win a World Series? Nobody knows. I'd like to think so, but sports have shown us time and again that plenty of good teams don't win championships. That for whatever reason even the strongest on paper and the strongest throughout the course of a full season often can't bring together the right mix of peak play and luck at the right time of the year.

But I also like that I'm even thinking in this context. I like that the turnstiles at PNC Park are again turning so much they need oiled regularly, the Bucs having drawn over two million fans in 2015. I like that Pittsburgh is developing a reputation as a desirable destination among Major League players. The mix of stadium atmosphere, team chemistry, and coaching ability to resurrect so many careers has become a tremendous selling point, in contrast to the days when being dealt to or signed by Pittsburgh was the last thing a player wanted.

I like a lot of things about the current state of Pirates baseball, none of which two consecutive years of frustrating Wild Card losses can take away. Most meaningfuly, I like that I was along for the entire ride, through all of the twists and turns, the ups and downs and definitely the detours, that the Pirates took to get to where they are today.

One Last Thing...

Thank you for reading this book; I hope you enjoyed it! If you did, there is one huge favor that I'd ask of you.

Please leave a review of the book on Amazon. Reviews help other potential readers decide if a book is something they'd be interested in and are a big part of helping authors get visibility on their work.

It doesn't take very long; just log in to your Amazon account and go to this book in your purchases, then publish your review.

Thank you again for reading!

Jason

42276171R00054

Made in the USA
Middletown, DE
06 April 2017